Weave a
Garment of
Brightness

Weave a Garment of Brightness

A Gathering of Prayers from Around the World

WAYNE LEE JONES

B

BERKLEY BOOKS, NEW YORK

To my sister, Kelly,
whose every act is a prayer
for the preservation of our earth.

Contents

$\mathcal{I}$ntroduction

Prayer is a process of articulation; it consists of putting in order thoughts, feelings, and needs with the intention of communicating them to some Other, whether this Other be God, one's own inner self, or a religious community. Prayer can happen silently, in the quiet of the mind. It can happen in speech and song and dance, in the company of multitudes. There are as many forms of prayer as there are human hearts, as many prayers as people to create them. So many, in fact, and of such diverse kinds, that it is sometimes hard to see how there can be a single thing called "prayer" at all.

This book is an attempt to capture the central experience of prayer through the presentation of some of these diverse forms. Some of the prayers in this book, such as the prayer of Thomas Aquinas, were meant as private meditations for personal transformation. Others, congregational prayers, are traditionally used in public to communicate the principles of religion or impart a common dream to the assembled congregants; the Jewish prayers in this book, for example, come from the daily prayer book. Still others offer explanations for difficult situations for the benefit of the community, and serve as verbalizations of the troubles of whole populations; the prayer of the Kung Bushmen is one example. Some prayers are praises of a god, lush descriptions that recount the attributes of the Divine, whether to instruct or simply to arouse feelings of love and devotion. The prayer of Surdas falls into this group. Other prayers give us insight into the nature of prayer by showing us how animals or even inanimate objects might pray; the work of Carl Sandburg and Carmen Bernos de Gasztold have this intention. But all of these prayers share some quality that unites them, though their time, place, and purpose of authorship are very different. They all communicate a need that is felt deeply and inwardly by the one who prays. They articulate clearly what may have been hidden, so that both the one who prays and the one who hears prayer can know clearly what is needed.

We find that for which we search when we examine other people's prayers. Those readers who treasure their own relationship with the Divine, by whatever name, will find their experience affirmed and elaborated upon in the prayers collected here. Further, some of the prayers included in this book are intended to serve as models of forms of devotional experience unfamiliar to most people in the West: the harsh rebuke of the ancestor spirits from the Zulu community is one such prayer. In language that might be considered inappropriate for religious discourse in the West, the Zulus express their frustration and redefine the mutual obligations incumbent upon both the spirits and the Zulus themselves. From another perspective, readers searching for a greater understanding of themselves will find value in the power of these prayers to expose the true feelings and needs that are behind the words. Certainly, readers looking to these prayers for their aesthetic and poetic qualities will not be disappointed; all of these prayers are beautiful and multidimensional.

The prayers collected in this book are arranged in three groups: petitions, praises, and prayers of thanksgiving. While all of the prayers in this anthology have numerous levels of interpretation and intention, they have been grouped in this manner for the convenience of readers who are searching for prayers that suit their particular needs. Praises are prayers that have as their primary purpose the enumeration of Divine attributes or the glorification of the Divine, whether motivated by didactic intentions or by exuberant love for a Deity. Petitions are, simply, prayers that ask for things. Part of the purpose of this collection is to show that different people ask for many different "things," both physical and spiritual. Finally, prayers of thanksgiving express gratitude for gifts received; these gifts may be perceived inwardly or outwardly; continually renewed, or the result of some peculiar grace. The Zulu prayer mentioned above is included in this section because it is like a prayer of thanksgiving in reverse; though its words do not outwardly express thanks, they reveal an awareness of interaction between the physical and the spiritual realms that is shared by many of the other prayers of thanksgiving included in this anthology.

A word to readers who pray themselves: I have made a special effort to ensure that the prayers collected here are ones that I could imagine myself praying. Indeed, a few of the prayers in this book are from my own hand. All of them have unique qualities; they speak to many different personalities and backgrounds and needs. Perhaps some of the prayers collected here will become favorites in your own devotions. Perhaps they will inspire you to create new and beautiful prayers of your own.

This is a book that I hope will be treasured and returned to again and again. It is a marvelous window into the spiritual experience of many different human beings, each with his or her own vision, hopes, and dreams. The voices collected here come from a wide range of times and places. Yet they show us something that in this day is becoming of pressing importance: that all human beings who pray have a common desire to express and articulate their needs and their understanding. Perhaps this book will in some small way contribute to a growing appreciation for that common desire, and help everyone who reads it see the common thread within the many different fabrics of religion.

PRAYERS

OF

PETITION

God
Let this be my prayer
before praying:
May my words be as sweet
as the honey of flowers
as sugar drunk from the heart of fresh cane.
May you strengthen my voice to bear
the weight of sincere prayer.
May you strengthen my mind to know clearly
why I pray.
May you strengthen my spirit with resolve
to complete my prayer without shame.
May you break my heart with an awareness
of the One
to whom I pray.

Wayne Lee Jones

O our Mother the Earth, O our Father the Sky,
Your children are we, and with tired backs
We bring you the gifts that you love.
Then weave for us a garment of brightness;
May the warp be the white light of morning,
May the weft be the red light of evening,
May the fringes be the falling rain,
May the border be the standing rainbow.
Thus weave for us a garment of brightness
That we may walk fittingly where birds sing,
That we may walk fittingly where grass is green,
O our Mother the Earth, O our Father the Sky!

"Song of the Sky Loom," a prayer of the Tewa tribe of the American Southwest

May all living beings have happiness and its cause;
May all living beings be separated from suffering
and its cause;
May they never be separated from that happiness
which is beyond suffering;
And may they abide in that equanimity which is
without attraction to the near or aversion to
the far.

A prayer of the Tibetan Buddhists

O God,
who art the unsearchable abyss of peace,
the ineffable sea of love,
the fountain of blessings
and the bestower of affection,
who sendest peace to those that receive it;
open to us this day the sea of thy love,
and water us with plenteous streams from the riches
    of Thy grace
and from the most sweet springs of thy benignity.
Make us children of quietness and heirs of peace.
Enkindle in us the fire of thy love;
sow in us thy fear;
strengthen our weakness by thy power;
bind us closely to thee and to each other
in one firm and indissoluble bond of unity.
Amen.

From the Syrian Clementine Liturgy

Father, O mighty force,
That force which is in everything,
Come down between us, fill us,
Until we be like thee,
Until we be like thee.

A prayer said during a boy's initiation in Guinea

Make us, O Lord, to flourish
like pure lilies in the courts of Thine house,
and to show forth to the faithful
the fragrance of good works,
and the example of a godly life,
through Thy mercy and grace.
Amen.

From the Mozarabic Sacramentary, an early Christian prayer book

Creator! You who dwell at the ends of the earth
unrivaled, you who gave being and power to men,
saying: let this be man, and to women, saying:
let this be woman! So saying, you made them,
     shaped them,
gave them being. These you created; watch over
     them!
Let them be safe and well, unharmed, living in
     peace.
Where are you? Up in the sky? Or down below?
In clouds? In storms? Hear me, answer me,
     acknowledge me,
give us perpetual life, hold us forever within your
     hand.
Receive this offering wherever you are.
Creator!

A prayer of the Inca people of Peru

Let us not run the world hastily,
Let us not grasp at the rope of wealth impatiently;
What should be treated with mature judgement,
Let us not treat in a fit of temper;
Whenever we arrive at a cool place,
Let us rest sufficiently well;
Let us give prolonged attention to the future,
And then let us give due regard to the consequence
    of things,
And that is on account of our sleeping.

A prayer of the Yoruba people of Africa

Grant unto me, O Lord, that with peace of mind I
may face all that this new day is to bring.

Grant unto me to dedicate myself completely to Thy
Holy Will.

For every hour of this day, instruct and support me
in all things.

Whatsoever tidings I may receive during the day, do
Thou teach me to accept tranquilly, in the firm
conviction that all eventualities fulfill Thy Holy
Will.

Govern Thou my thoughts and feelings in all I do
and say.

When things unforeseen occur, let me not forget
that all cometh down from Thee.

Teach me to behave sincerely and rationally toward
every member of my family, that I may bring
confusion and sorrow to none.

Bestow upon me, my Lord, strength to endure the
fatigue of the day, and to bear my part in all its
passing events.

Guide Thou my will and teach me to pray, to
believe, to hope, to suffer, to forgive, and to
love.

Amen.

A private meditation used in the Eastern Orthodox Church

O God, do thou thine ear incline,
Protect my children and my kine,
E'en if thou'rt weary, still forbear,
And hearken to my constant prayer.
When shrouded 'neath the cloak of night,
Thy splendours sleep beyond our sight,
And when across the sky by day,
Thou movest, still to thee I pray.
Dread shades of our departed sires,
Ye who can make or mar desires,
Slain by no mortal hand ye dwell,
Beneath the earth, O guard us well.

A prayer of the Nandi people of Africa

Kirinyaga, owner of all things,
I pray thee, give me what I need,
Because I am suffering,
And also my children are suffering
And all things that are in this country of mine.
I beg thee for life,
The good one with things,
Healthy people with no disease,
May they bear healthy children.
And also to women who suffer because they are
        barren,
Open the way by which they may see children.
Give goats, cattle, food, honey,
And also the troubles of the other lands
That I do not know, remove.

A prayer of the Meru people of Africa

Lord, make me an instrument of thy peace.
Where there is hatred, let me sow love;
where there is injury, pardon;
where there is doubt, faith;
where there is despair, hope;
where there is darkness, light;
where there is sadness, joy.
O Divine Master, grant that I may not so much
    seek to be consoled, as to console;
to be understood, as to understand;
to be loved, as to love.
For it is in giving, that we receive;
it is in pardoning, that we are pardoned;
it is in dying, that we are born to eternal life.

A personal prayer of St. Francis of Assisi

When the heart is hard and parched up,
Come upon me with a shower of mercy.
When grace is lost from life,
Come with a burst of song.
When tumultuous work raises its din on all sides
     shutting me out from beyond,
     Come to me, my Lord of silence, with thy
     peace and rest.
When my beggarly heart sits crouched, shut up in a
     corner,
Break open the door, my king, and come with the
     ceremony of a king.
When desire blinds the mind with delusion and
     dust,
O thou holy One, thou wakeful,
Come with thy light and thy thunder.

From the Gitanjali of Rabindranath Tagore

O Great Spirit, whose voice I hear in the wind,
And whose breath gives life to all the world,
Hear me—I come before you, one of your many
     children.
I am small and weak; I need your strength and
     wisdom.

Let me walk in beauty and make my eyes ever
     behold the red and purple sunset;
Make my hands respect the things you have made,
     my ears sharp to hear your voice.
Make me wise so that I may know the things you
     have taught my people;
The lesson you have hidden in every leaf and rock.

I seek strength not to be superior to my brother,
But to be able to fight my greatest enemy—myself.
Make me ever ready to come to you with clean
     hands and straight eyes,
So when life fades as a fading sunset, my spirit may
     come to you without shame.

A prayer of the Dakota tribe of the American Great Plains

Give me, O Lord, a steadfast heart,
which no unworthy affection may drag downwards;
give me an unconquered heart,
which no tribulation can wear out;
give me an upright heart,
which no unworthy purpose may tempt aside.
Bestow on me also, O Lord, my God,
understanding to know you,
diligence to seek you,
wisdom to find you,
and a faithfulness that may finally embrace you,
through Jesus Christ our Lord,
Amen.

A personal prayer of St. Thomas Aquinas

May all I say and all I think
Be in harmony with thee,
God within me,
God beyond me,
maker of the trees.

A prayer of the Chinook tribe of the Pacific Northwest

Though I am far from You,
May no one else be far from You.

A prayer of the Persian poet Hafiz

May I become a medicine for the sick and their
       physician, their support until sickness come not
       again.
May I become an unfailing store for the wretched,
       and be first to supply them with their needs.
My own self and my pleasures, my righteousness
       past, present, and future, may I sacrifice
       without regard, in order to achieve the welfare
       of beings.

A prayer of the Hindu mystic Santideva

Come to my help, O Ram,
Come to my help, dear Ram.

Whether amongst men, or in forest wild, I have none
but Thee.
I have no one in my heart or eye but Thee.

Come to my help, O Ram,
Come to my help, dear Ram.

Thou art my relatives, my mother and father
Thou alone art my heart and my wealth.

Come to my help, O Ram,
Come to my help, dear Ram.

Aside from Thee I know no one,
Whom I at all recognize as my helper.

Come to my help, O Ram,
Come to my help, dear Ram.

In body, speech, and in the feelings of my heart,
I find everlasting happiness in Thy name.

Come to my help, O Ram,
Come to my help, dear Ram.

Without Thy constant presence,
Where can Dinkar find a place of rest?

Come to my help, O Ram,
Come to my help, dear Ram.

A prayer of the Hindu poet Dinkar

Lord of the springtime, Father of flower,
field and fruit, smile on us in these
earnest days when the work is heavy and
the toil wearisome; lift up our hearts,
O God, to the things worthwhile—
sunshine and night, the dripping rain,
the song of the birds, books and music,
and the voices of our friends. Lift up
our hearts to these this night, O Father,
and grant us Thy peace.

From Prayers for Dark People *by W. E. B. Du Bois*

Through the virtue of this effort to enter
Into the ways leading to enlightenment,
May all living beings
Come to engage in those conducts.

May all beings everywhere
Plagued with sufferings of body and mind
Obtain an ocean of happiness and joy
By virtue of my merits.

For as long as they remain in cyclic existence
May their happiness never decline,
And may all of them uninterruptedly receive
Waves of joy from Bodhisattvas.

May all embodied creatures
Who throughout the universe
Experience hellish realms
Come to enjoy the bliss of Sukhavati.

May those feeble with cold find warmth,
And may those oppressed with heat be cooled
By the boundless waters that pour forth
From the great clouds of the Bodhisattva.

May the forest of razor sharp leaves
Become a beautiful pleasure grove,
And may the trees of knives and swords
Grow into wish-fulfilling trees.

May the regions of hell become places of joy
With vast and fragrant lotus pools
Beautified with the exquisite calls
Of wild ducks, geese, and swans.

May the heaps of burning coals turn into heaps of jewels,
May the burning ground become a polished crystal
    floor,
And may the mountains of the crushing hells
Become a celestial palace of worship filled with
    Sugatas.

May the rains of lava, blazing stones and weapons
From now on become a rain of flowers,
And may all battling with weapons
From now on be a playful exchange of flowers.

A prayer of the Tibetan Buddhists

O Lord, be gracious unto us! In all that we hear or
see, in all that we say or do, be gracious unto
us.

I ask pardon of the Great God. I ask pardon at the
sunset, when every sinner turns to Him. Now
and for ever I ask pardon of God. O Lord,
cover us from our sins, guard our children and
protect our weaker friends.

A traditional prayer of the Bedouin people of the Arabian Peninsula,
recited at sunset

O Lord our God,
grant us grace to desire you with our whole heart,
that so desiring we may seek and find you,
and so finding you, may love you,
and loving you, may hate those sins
from which you have redeemed us.

A prayer of St. Anselm

O Merciful God, be Thou now unto me a strong
    tower of defence, I humbly entreat Thee. Give
    me grace to await Thy leisure, and patiently to
    bear what Thou doest unto me; nothing
    doubting or mistrusting Thy goodness towards
    me; for Thou knowest what is good for me
    better than I do. Therefore do with me in all
    things that Thou wilt; only arm me, I beseech
    Thee, with Thine armor, that I may stand fast,
    above all things, taking to me the shield of
    faith; praying always that I may refer myself
    wholly to Thy will, abiding Thy pleasure, and
    comforting myself in those troubles which it
    shall please Thee to send me, seeing such
    troubles are profitable for me; and I am
    assuredly persuaded that all Thou doest cannot
    but be well; and unto Thee be all honor and
    glory. Amen.

A prayer composed by Lady Jane Grey on the eve of her execution

Grandfather, Great Spirit, you have been always,
and before you no one has been.
There is no other one to pray to but you.
You yourself, everything that you see, everything has
      been made by you.
The star nations all over the universe you have
      finished.
The four quarters of the earth you have finished.
The day, and in that day, everything you have
      finished.

Grandfather, Great Spirit, lean close to the earth
that you may hear the voice I send.
You towards where the sun goes down, behold me;
Thunder Beings, behold me!
You where the White Giant lives in power, behold
      me!
You where the sun shines continually,
whence come the day-break star and the day, behold
      me!
You where the summer lives, behold me!
You in the depths of the heavens, an eagle of power,
      behold!
And you, Mother Earth, the only Mother,
you who have shown mercy to your children!

Hear me, four quarters of the world—a relative I am!
Give me the strength to walk the soft earth, a
        relative to all that is!
Give me the eyes to see and the strength to
        understand, that I may be like you.
With your power only can I face the winds.

Great Spirit, Great Spirit, my Grandfather, all over the
        earth
the faces of living things are all alike.
With tenderness have these come up out of the
        ground.
Look upon these faces of children without number
and with children in their arms,
that they may face the winds
and walk the good road to the day of quiet.

A prayer of the Native American holy man Black Elk

If I, O Indra, were, like you, the single Sovereign of all wealth, my worshipper would be rich in cattle.

I would be pleased, O Lord of Power, to strengthen and enrich the sage, were I the Lord of herds of cattle.

To worshippers who press the juice, your goodness, Indra, is a cow, yielding in plenty cattle and steeds.

None is there, Indra, God or man, to hinder your munificence, the wealth which, lauded, you will give.

The sacrifice made Indra strong when he unrolled the earth, and made himself a diadem in heaven.

Your aid we claim, O Indra, you who after you have waxed great, have won all treasures for your own.

In Soma's ecstasy Indra spread the firmament and realms of light, when he cleft Vala limb from limb.

Showing the hidden he drove forth the cows for the Angirases, and Vala he cast headlong down.

By Indra were the luminous realms of heaven established and secured, firm and immovable from their place.

Indra, your praise moves quickly like a joyous wave
 of water: bright shine the drops that gladden
 you.

For you, O Indra, are the God whom hymns and
 praises magnify; you bless those who worship
 you.

Let the two long-maned Bay Steeds bring Indra to
 drink the Soma juice, the Bountiful to our
 sacrifice.

With waters' foam you tore off, Indra, the head of
 Namuchi, subduing all contending hosts.

The Dasyus, when they sought to climb by magic
 arts and mount to heaven, you, Indra, cast
 down to earth.

As Soma-drinker conquering all, you scatter to
 every side their settlement who poured no
 gifts.

Hymn 8:14 from the Rig Veda, *a central text of Hinduism*

O Lord, grant us to love Thee; grant that we may
    love those that love Thee;
grant that we may do
the deeds that win Thy love.
Make the love of Thee be dearer to us than
    ourselves,
than our families, than wealth, and even
than cool water.

A saying of the Prophet Muhammad, founder of Islam

From the unreal lead me to the real.
From darkness lead me to light.
From death lead me to immortality.

From the Upanishads, texts from the Hindu tradition

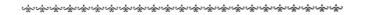

All that I ought to have thought and have not
thought;
All that I ought to have said and have not said;
All that I ought to have done and have not done;
All that I ought not to have thought and yet have
thought;
All that I ought not to have spoken and yet have
spoken;
All that I ought not to have done and yet have
done;
For thoughts, words, and works, I pray for
forgiveness and repent with penance.

From the Zend-Avesta, *a central text of Zoroastrianism*

O Lord, let us not live to be useless.

A prayer of John Wesley, founder of the Methodist Church

Gauwa must help us that we kill an animal.
Gauwa, help us. We are dying of hunger.
Gauwa does not give us help.
He is cheating. He is bluffing.
Gauwa will bring something for us to kill next day
After he himself hunts and has eaten meat,
When he is full and is feeling well.

A prayer of the Kung Bushmen of Africa

Use me then, my Saviour,
for whatever purpose, and in whatever way,
you may require.
Here is my poor heart, an empty vessel;
fill it with your grace.
Here is my sinful and troubled soul;
quicken it and refresh it with your love.
Take my heart for your abode;
my mouth to spread abroad the glory of your name;
my love and all my powers, for the advancement of
your believing people;
and never suffer the steadfastness and confidence of
my faith to abate;
so that at all times I may be enabled from the heart
to say,
"Jesus needs me, and I am his."

A prayer of the American evangelist Dwight L. Moody

May the wicked become good.
May the good obtain peace.
May the peaceful be freed from bonds.
May the freed set others free.

Blessings on the subjects of those who are ruling,
and may these great lords rule the earth in a just
    manner.
May good always be the lot of cows and brahmins.
May all people be happy.

May it rain at the right time.
May the earth have storehouses full of grain.
May this country be free of disturbances.
May brahmins be free of persecution.

May all be happy.
May all be healthy.
May all see only auspicious sights.
May no one have a share in sorrow.

May everyone surmount his difficulties.
May everyone see only auspicious sights.
May everyone have his desires fulfilled.
May everyone everywhere be glad.

May blessings fall on our mother and father;
blessings on the cows, the fields, the workers.
May everything of ours flourish and be an aid to
    knowledge.
And long may we see the sun.

Om. Peace! Peace! Peace!

The "Universal Prayer," from the daily chants of the Siddha Yoga Dham Foundation

In Tsegihi

In the house made of dawn,

In the house made of evening twilight,

In the house made of dark cloud,

In the house made of rain and mist, of pollen, of
grasshoppers,

The path to which is on the rainbow,

Where the zigzag lightning stands high on top,

O male divinity!

With your moccasins of dark cloud, come to us. . . .

With the far darkness made of the rain and the
mist. . . .

With the zigzag lightning, with the rainbow
hanging high on the ends of your wings, come
to us, soaring.

With the darkness on the earth, come to us.

With these I wish the foam floating on the flowing
water over the roots of the great corn. . . .

Happily may fair yellow corn, fair blue corn, fair
corn of all kinds, plants of all kinds, to the
ends of the earth, come with you. . . .

Thus you accomplish your tasks.

Happily the old men will regard you,

The young men and the young women will regard
you,

The children will regard you. . . .
May their roads home be on the trail of peace,
Happily may they all return.
In beauty I walk,
With beauty before me I walk,
With beauty behind me I walk,
With beauty above me and about me, I walk.
It is finished in beauty.
It is finished in beauty.

"Hymn to the Thunderbird," a prayer of the Navajo tribe of the
American Southwest

Fix thou our steps, O Lord,
that we stagger not at the uneven motions of the
world,
but steadily go on to our glorious home;
neither censuring our journey by the weather we
meet with,
nor turning out of the way for anything that befalls
us.
The winds are often rough,
and our own weight presses us downwards.
Reach forth, O Lord, thy hand,
thy saving hand,
and speedily deliver us.
Teach us, O Lord, to use this transitory life
as pilgrims returning to their beloved home;
that we may take what our journey requires,
and not think of settling in a foreign country.

A prayer of John Wesley, founder of the Methodist Church

God bless the field and bless the furrow,
Stream and branch and rabbit burrow,
Hill and stone and flower and tree,
From Bristol town to Wetherby—
Bless the sun and bless the sleet,
Bless the lane and bless the street,
Bless the night and bless the day,
From Somerset and all the way
To the meadows of Cathay;
Bless the minnow, bless the whale,
Bless the rainbow and the hail,
Bless the nest and bless the leaf,
Bless the righteous and the thief,
Bless the wing and bless the fin,
Bless the air I travel in,
Bless the mill and bless the mouse,
Bless the miller's bricken house,
Bless the earth and bless the sea,
God bless you and God bless me.

A traditional English prayer

I am only a spark
Make me a fire.
I am only a string
Make me a lyre.
I am only a drop
Make me a fountain.
I am only an ant hill
Make me a mountain.
I am only a feather
Make me a wing.
I am only a rag
Make me a King!

Amado Nervo

Teach me, God, to pray
in laughter as much as in words
to delight in the world of sense and feeling
that is Yours, that is Your garment.

Teach me, God, to pray
in tears as much as in words
to shed my tears to You, consciously,
in times of sincere frustration.

Teach me, God, to pray
in works as much as in words
to make my actions thoughtful messages
to make my actions more beautiful than words.

Teach me, God, to pray
in a way that is pleasing to you
in a way that is more than an appeasement
of my fears.

Wayne Lee Jones

Perhaps in a past life to benefit beings
I made great efforts in difficult practices
And sacrificed even my own happiness for them.
If so, may this cause the doctrine to flourish for
    long.

Perhaps in a past life to benefit the sick
I dedicated even the necessities of life
To protect living beings from weakness and sorrow.
If so, may this cause the doctrine to flourish for
    long.

Perhaps in a past life to accomplish enlightenment
I renounced sons, daughters, wives,
Wealth, elephants, and chariots.
If so, may this cause the doctrine to flourish for
    long.

Perhaps I once made auspicious offerings
To the Fully Awakened Buddhas, the
    Pratyekabuddhas,
Sravaka Arhants or my elders.
If so, may this cause the doctrine to flourish for
    long.

Perhaps in the past for countless aeons
I underwent endless hardships and trials
In the search for the meaning of true
     enlightenment.
If so, may this cause the doctrine to flourish for
     long.

Perhaps I once practiced discipline and penance,
Applied myself to the austere yogas,
Or devoted myself to a Buddha of the ten directions.
If so, may this cause the doctrine to flourish for
     long.

Perhaps I once exerted great perseverance
And through constance in practice overcame a fault.
If so, may this cause the doctrine to flourish for
     long,
That countless living beings may attain to freedom.

A prayer of the Tibetan Buddhists

Lover of our souls,
Come into these cold and empty hearts of ours,
Come to fill them with light, warmth, and love,
With the heavenly music,
With the sound of the eternal harmony,
With the footfalls of the saints that rejoice in Thy
     bliss;
Thou art Lord of all, Master of suns and stars,
Yet art Thou our Beloved,
The Saviour of our souls from death and night.

Come, our Lord, Thou Lover of our souls,
Come to purify and uplift our failing hearts,
Come to impart unto us the eternal joy of those
     that are in bliss with Thee.

John S. Hoyland

Lord most giving and resourceful,
I implore you:
make it your will
that this people enjoy
the goods and riches you naturally give,
that naturally issue from you,
that are pleasing and savory,
that delight and comfort,
though lasting but briefly,
passing away as if in a dream.

A prayer of the Aztec people of Mexico

Who is so low that I am not his brother?
Who is so high that I've no path to him?
Who is so poor I may not feel his hunger?
Who is so rich I may not pity him?

Who is so hurt I may not know his heartache?
Who sings for joy my heart may never share?
Who in God's heaven has passed beyond my vision?
Who to hell's depths where I may never fare?

May none, then, call on me for understanding,
May none, then, turn to me for help in pain,
And drain alone his bitter cup of sorrow,
Or find he knocks upon my heart in vain.

S. Ralph Harlow

My Lord, I know not what I ought to ask of Thee.
Thou and Thou alone knowest my needs.
Thou lovest me more than I am able to love Thee.
O Father, grant unto me, Thy servant, all which I
    cannot ask.
For a cross I dare not ask, nor for consolation;
I dare only to stand in Thy presence.
My heart is open to Thee.
Thou seest my needs of which I myself am unaware.
Behold and lift me up!
In Thy presence I stand,
awed and silenced by Thy will and Thy judgments,
into which my mind cannot penetrate.
To Thee I offer myself as a sacrifice.
No other desire is mine but to fulfill Thy will.
Teach me how to pray.
Do Thyself pray within me.
Amen.

A prayer of Philaret, Metropolitan of Moscow

I wish, O Son of the living God, ancient and eternal
  King, for a secret hut in the wilderness that it
  may be my dwelling.
A very blue shallow well to be beside it, a clear pool
  for washing away sins through the grace of the
  Holy Ghost.
A beautiful wood close by around it on every side,
  for the nurture of many-voiced birds, to shelter
  and hide it.
Facing the south for warmth, a little stream across
  its enclosure, a choice ground with abundant
  bounties which would be good for every plant.
A few sage disciples, I will tell their number, humble
  and obedient, to pray to the King.
Four threes, three fours, fit for every need, two sixes
  in the church both south and north.
Six couples in addition to me myself, praying
  through the long ages to the King who moves
  the sun.
A lovely church decked with linen, a dwelling for
  God of Heaven; then, bright candles over the
  holy white Scriptures.
One room to go to for the care of the body, without
  wantonness, without voluptuousness, without
  meditation of evil.

This is the housekeeping I would undertake, I would
     choose it without concealing: fragrant fresh
     leeks, hens, speckled salmon, bees.
My fill of clothing and of food from the King of
     good fame, and for me to be sitting for a while
     praying to God in every place.

"The Wish of Manchan of Liath," a traditional Celtic prayer

Our eyes may see some uncleanness, but let not our
    mind see things that are not clean.
Our ears may hear some uncleanness, but let not
    our mind hear things that are not clean.

A Shinto prayer from Japan

Teach me, O God, not to torture myself,
not to make a martyr out of myself,
through stifling reflection,
but rather teach me to breathe deeply in faith.

A personal prayer of the theologian and philosopher Søren Kierkegaard

May obedience conquer disobedience within this
    house,
and may peace triumph over discord here,
and generous giving over avarice,
reverence over contempt,
speech with truthful words over lying utterance;
may the righteous order gain the victory
over the demon of the lie.

From the Yasna, *a text from the Zoroastrian tradition*

Bless to me, O God, the moon that is above me,
Bless to me, O God, the earth that is beneath me,
Bless to me, O God, my wife and my children,
And bless, O God, myself who have care of them;
    Bless to me my wife and my children,
    And bless, O God, myself who have care of
    them.

Bless, O God, the thing on which mine eye doth rest,
Bless, O God, the thing on which my hope doth
    rest,
Bless, O God, my reason and my purpose,
Bless, O bless Thou them, Thou God of life;
    Bless, O God, my reason and my purpose,
    Bless, O bless Thou them, Thou God of life.

Bless to me the bed-companion of my love,
Bless to me the handling of my hands,
Bless, O bless Thou to me, O God, the fencing of
    my defence,
And bless, O bless to me the angeling of my rest;
    Bless, O bless Thou to me, O God, the fencing
    of my defence,
    And bless, O bless to me the angeling of my
    rest.

A traditional Celtic prayer, collected by Alexander Carmichael

To gain the reward of good deeds and to win
    forgiveness for my sins,
I perform Righteous acts for the love of my Soul.
May all good deeds of all good men throughout the
    seven spheres,
get their share of blessings,
wide as the earth,
extensive as the rivers,
exalted as the Sun!
May you be Righteous and long-lived!
So may it be!

A Zoroastrian prayer

Lord, not for light in darkness do we pray,
Not that the veil be lifted from our eyes,
Nor that the slow ascension of our day
    Be otherwise.

Not for a clearer vision of the things
Whereof the fashioning shall make us great,
Not for remission of the peril and stings
    Of time and fate.

Not for a fuller knowledge of the end
Whereto we travel, bruised yet unafraid,
Nor that the little healing that we lend
    Shall be repaid.

Not these, O Lord. We would not break the bars
Thy wisdom sets about us; we shall climb
Unfetter'd to the secrets of the stars
    In Thy good time.

We do not crave the high perception swift
When to refrain were well, and when fulfil,
Nor yet the understanding strong to sift
    The good from ill.

Not these, O Lord. For these Thou hast reveal'd,
We know the golden season when to reap
The heavy-fruited treasure of the field,
    The hour to sleep.

Not these. We know the hemlock from the rose,
The pure from stain'd, the noble from the base,
The tranquil holy light of truth that glows
  On Pity's face.

We know the paths wherein our feet should press,
Across our hearts are written Thy decrees:
Yet now, O Lord, be merciful to bless
  With more than these.

Grant us the will to fashion as we feel,
Grant us the strength to labour as we know,
Grant us the purpose, ribb'd and edged with steel,
  To strike the blow.

Knowledge we ask not—knowledge Thou hast lent,
But, Lord, the will—there lies our bitter need,
Give us to build above the deep intent
  The deed, the deed.

John Drinkwater

And now may God, the Soul of the Universe,
Be pleased with this my offering of words,
And being pleased may He give me
This favour in return.

That the crookedness of evil men may cease,
And that the love of goodness may grow in them.
May all beings experience from one another
The friendship of the heart.
May the darkness of sin disappear.
May the Universe see the rising of the Sun of
        Righteousness.
Whatever is desired, may it be received
By every living being.

May He bless the multitude of those who love God
And shower on men all forms of blessings;
May they constantly, on this earth,
Come in touch with its living beings.

May this forest of walking Wish-trees,
May this city built of living Wish-gems,
May this talking sea of nectar,
May these moons without dark spots,
May these suns without fierce heat,
May all these ever-good men,
Be the close kin of mankind.

And now in every form of happiness
May there be enjoyment to the full everywhere.
And may the Supreme Being be worshipped
For ever and ever.

A prayer of the Hindu poet Dñayaneshvari

Dear God, give me time.
Men are always so driven!
Make them understand that I can never hurry.
Give me time to eat.
Give me time to plod.
Give me time to sleep.
Give me time to think.

"The Prayer of the Ox," by Carmen Bernos de Gasztold

As a fish that is dragged from the water gaspeth,
So gaspeth my soul:

As one who hath buried his treasure,
And now cannot find the place,
So is my mind distraught:

As a child that hath lost its mother,
So am I troubled, my heart is seared with sore
     anguish:

O merciful God,
Thou knowest my need,
Come, save me, and show me Thy love.

A prayer of the Hindu mystic Tukaram

May I follow a life of compassion in pity for
the suffering of all living things. Teach me to live
with reverence for life everywhere, to treat life as
sacred, and respect all that breathes. O Father,
I grope amid the shadows of doubt and fear, but I
long to advance toward the light. Help me to fling
my life like a flaming firebrand into the gathering
darkness of the world.

A prayer of Dr. Albert Schweitzer

Lay me on an anvil, O God.
Beat me and hammer me into a crowbar.
Let me pry loose old walls.
Let me lift and loosen old foundations.

Lay me on an anvil, O God.
Beat me and hammer me into a steel spike.
Drive me into the girders that hold a skyscraper
together.
Take red-hot rivets and fasten me into the central
girders.
Let me be the great nail holding a skyscraper
through blue nights into white stars.

"Prayers of Steel" by Carl Sandburg

Forgive us, God,
for prayers that do not thank
for prayers that are not praises
for prayers that beg of You the least of our wants,
omitting our greatest needs.

Forgive us, God,
when we pray for what we know we should not
     have
when we pray for what we can do ourselves
when we pray for what we already have
but have forgotten.
Forgive us, God,
for prayers that deny the abundance of Your gifts,
for placing our names
before Your own.

Wayne Lee Jones

PRAYERS

OF

PRAISE

You sit on a lotus seat of strong effort,
Its lotus roots of aspiration firm
In the ground of faith fully developed,
Venerable Tara—homage to You!

You sit on a moon seat, cooling with compassion
Migrating beings scorched by the heat of
    defilements.
Goddess, Saviouress of tormented beings,
Venerable Tara—homage to You!

With the two accumulations as chariot-wheels
You've conquered the two veils; established in the
    Ten Stages,
You stay as Goddess until samsara is empty,
Venerable Tara—homage to You!

Your body, unmoved by defilements, is firm like a
    mountain,
Well-grown, since nourished by Your perfect
    virtues,
Full-breasted, since loving-kindness moves Your
    heart,
Venerable Tara—homage to You!

Graceful, Your complexion unstained by samsara;
Of charming apparel, with jewel ornaments,
Your hair blue-green, with a diadem of the five
    Families,
Venerable Tara—homage to You!

Your smiling face spreads uncontaminate bliss;
Born of Vairocana, You have compassion and deeds.
With Wisdom's and Means' bow and arrow
    subduing the Maras,
Venerable Tara—homage to You!

Right hand giving Refuge, You save from fears;
In the form of a maid of sixteen, You captivate
    beings;
Your blue utpala is for the Action Family,
Venerable Tara—homage to You!

You are the skillful boatman who carries us over
The rivers of rebirth, aging, sickness, and death
To the harbour of loving-kindness, with oars of
    compassion,
Venerable Tara—homage to You!

Now that I have praised the Goddess so,
In eight stanzas, with faith in Her, through this
May every migrating sentient being
Quickly win the rank of Buddhahood!

A Buddhist praise of the goddess Tara

From In Praise of Tara: Songs to the Saviouress; *Wisdom Publications*

Wisely have I enjoyed the savory drink, with
    religious thoughts, best to find out treasure.
The food to which all Deities and mortals, calling it
    meat, gather themselves together.
You will be called Aditi as you have entered within,
    appeaser of celestial anger.
Indu, enjoying Indra's friendship, bring us—as a
    swift steed the chariot—forward to riches.
We have drunk Soma and become immortal; we
    have attained the light, the Gods discovered.
Now what harm may a foe's malice do to us?
    What, O Immortal, mortal man's deception?
Absorbed into the heart, be sweet, O Indu, as a kind
    father to his son, O Soma,
As a wise Friend to a friend: O Soma, wide-ruler,
    lengthen out our days for living.
These glorious drops that give me freedom have I
    drunk.
Closely they knit my joints as straps secure a
    chariot.
Let them protect my foot from slipping on the way:
    yea, let the drops I drink preserve me from
    disease.
Make me shine bright like fire produced by friction:
    give us a clearer sight and make us better.
For in carouse I think of thee, O Soma, Shall I, as a
    rich man, attain to comfort?

May we enjoy with an enlivened spirit the juice
  thou givest, like ancestral riches.
O Soma, King, prolong our existence as Surya
  makes the shining days grow longer.
King Soma, favor us and make us prosper: we are
  thy devotees; of this be mindful.
Spirit and power are fresh in us, O Indu: give us not
  up to our foe's pleasure.
For you have settled in each joint, O Soma, aim of
  men's eyes and guardian of our bodies.
When we offend against thine holy statutes, as a
  kind Friend, God, best of all, be gracious.
May I be with the Friend whose heart is tender,
  who, Lord of Bays, when quaffed will never
  harm me—
This Soma now deposited within me. For this, I
  pray for longer life to Indra.
Our maladies have lost their strength and vanished:
  they feared, and passed away into the darkness.
Soma has risen in us, exceedingly mighty, and we
  are come where men prolong existence.
Fathers, that Indu which our hearts have drunk,
  Immortal in himself, has entered mortals.
So let us serve this Soma with oblation, and rest
  securely in his grace and favor.

O Soma, associate with the Fathers you have spread
    yourself abroad through earth and heaven.
So with oblation let us serve you, O Indu, and so
    let us become the lords of riches,
Give us your blessing, O Gods, preservers. Never
    may sleep or idle talk control us.
But evermore may we, as friends of Soma, speak to
    the congregation with brave sons around us.
On all sides, Soma, you are our life-giver: aim of all
    eyes, light-finder, come within us.
Indu, of one accord with your protections both
    from behind and from before preserve us.

A praise of the ritual drink Soma from the Rig Veda, *one of the
central texts of Hinduism*

You are my father and mother, You are my Lord.
You are loving uncle and aunt to me.
You are lovely woman and rich treasure,
my only family, friends, and home.
You give me the pleasures of this world
and the other, and save me in the end.
O sole friend who moves my heart to leave this
world,
O my gold and precious gems and pearls!
You are my God, my treasure who rides the bull!

A hymn of praise for Shiva from the Tamil people of southern India

Great Spirit!
Piler up of the rocks into towering mountains!
When thou stampest on the stone,
The dust rises and fills the land.
Hardness of the precipice;
Waters of the pool that turn
Into misty rain when stirred.
Vessel overflowing with oil!
Father of Runji,
Who seweth the heavens like cloth:
Let him knit together that which is below.
Caller forth of the branching trees:
Thou bringest forth the shoots
That they stand erect.
Thou hast filled the land with mankind,
The dust rises on high, oh Lord!
Wonderful One, thou livest
In the midst of the sheltering rocks,
Thou givest rain to mankind:
We pray to thee,
Hear us, Lord!
Show mercy when we beseech thee, Lord.
Thou art on high with the spirits of the great.
Thou raisest the grass-covered hills
Above the earth, and createst the rivers,
Gracious One.

A hymn of the Shona people of southern Africa

How many days have passed since You departed, my
　　　Beloved! I watch in wait for your coming!

My Lord, my Merciful one, my Kindly one, as I
　　　wait in hope for You, how will these days pass
　　　in Your absence, o Beloved?

Giving me His promise, my Lord went off to His
　　　city, o Beloved. So keep the promise of love
　　　which You gave.

Had I known all this, I would not have let You go,
　　　o Beloved, and I too would have gone with You.

How can the child whose parents have left their city
　　　remain behind, o Beloved?

Their child cries out, o Beloved, like a calf separated
　　　from its mother's teat.

Or like a fish separated from water, o Beloved.
　　　How long can it survive?

In the eddies of the water and the shadows of the
　　　flowers, o Beloved, forms of so many kinds
　　　have been created.

A fire is burning in my heart, o Beloved. You alone
　　　can quench it.

Grief and joy are both inscribed in one's destiny by
　　　the Lord, o Beloved, so do not blame anyone
　　　for these.

Let me touch Your feet, O let our glances meet, o
　　　Beloved. Let mercy enter Your heart.

A hymn of the Ismaili Muslims attributed to Pir Sadruddin

Lord,

Can I enumerate the works of your love?

You drive the sea against the shores

And push the mountains up from plains.

You cause the rain to seek the earth

And rivers fed with rain to seek the sea.

You make sweet the taste of fruits

And cause fruits to taste different from one another.

You make sweet the taste of our lover's kiss

And help us to hold our lover in our hearts like no
     other.

You make the green plant to love the sun

And the cloud to seek a home in the heights of the
     sky.

You cause East and West to seek each other
     perpetually in the spinning of the earth

And ignite tension between the poles North and
     South.

The works of your love are endless

But let me see them wherever I look

Let me see the operation of your love

Let me see the real pattern of your love

Beneath the apparent.

Wayne Lee Jones

He says: 'I declare in the presence of the sovereign
    gods of the harvest. If the sovereign gods will
    bestow in many-bundled ears and in luxuriant
    ears the late-ripening harvest which they will
    bestow, the late-ripening harvest which will be
    produced by the dripping of foam through the
    arms and by drawing the mud together
    between the opposing thighs, then I will fulfil
    their praises by setting up the first fruits in a
    thousand ears and many hundred ears, raising
    high the beer-jars, filling and ranging-in-rows
    the bellies of the beer-jars, I will present them
    in juice and in ear. As to things which grow
    in the great-field-plain—sweet herbs and bitter
    herbs: as to things which dwell in the blue-sea
    plain—things wide of fin and things narrow of
    fin, down to the weeds of the offing and weeds
    of the shore: and as to clothes—with bright
    cloth, glittering cloth, soft cloth and coarse
    cloth will I fulfil praises. And having furnished
    a white horse, a white boar and white cock,
    and the various kinds of things in the presence
    of the sovereign god of the harvest, I fulfil his
    praises by setting up the great offerings of the
    sovereign Grandchild's augustness.'

The text of a Shinto ritual offering from Japan

O most high almighty, good Lord God, to Thee
belong praise, glory, honour, and all blessing!

Praised be my Lord God with all His creatures; and
specially our brother the sun, who brings us the
day, and who brings us the light, fair is he, and
shining with a very great splendour.

Praised be my Lord for our sister the moon, and for the
stars which He has set clear and lovely in heaven.

Praised be my Lord for our brother the wind, and for
air and cloud, calms and all weather, by which
Thou upholdest in life all creatures.

Praised be my Lord for our sister water, who is very
serviceable unto us, and humble, and precious, and
clean.

Praised be my Lord for our brother fire, through whom
Thou givest us light in the darkness; and he is
bright and pleasant, and very mighty, and strong.

Praised be my Lord for our mother the earth, which
doth sustain us and keep us, and bringeth forth
divers fruits, and flowers of many colours, and
grass.

Praise ye, and bless ye the Lord, and give thanks
unto Him and serve Him with great humility.

The Song of the Sun, written by St. Francis of Assisi

I would be saved
    And I would save
I would be loosed
    And I would loose
I would be born
    And I would bear
I would hear
    And I would be heard
Grace danceth.
    I would pipe; dance ye all.
I would flee
    And I would stay
I would adorn
    And I would be adorned
I would be united
    And I would unite
A house I have not
    And I have houses
A place I have not
    And I have places
A temple I have not
    And I have temples
    A lamp am I to thee that beholdest me.
    A mirror am I to thee that perceivest me.
    A door am I to thee that knockest at me.
    A way am I to thee a wayfarer.

    Now answer to my dancing.

A spiritual dialogue between a worshipper and Christ, from the apocryphal
Acts of John

The heavens are wide, exceedingly wide.
The earth is wide, very, very wide.
We have lifted it and taken it away.
We have lifted it and brought it back.
From time immemorial,
The God of old bids us all
Abide by his injunctions.
Then shall we get whatever we want,
Be it white or red.
It is God, the Creator, the Gracious One.
Good morning to you, God, good morning.
I am learning, let me succeed.

A drum-song of the Akan people of Ghana

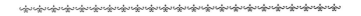

You are ever mighty,
Lord Who brings the dead to life,
You are great in granting salvation,
providing the living with sustenance with loving-
    kindness,
bringing the dead to life with great mercies,
supporting the fallen,
healing the sick,
releasing the captive,
and keeping faith with those asleep in the dust.
Who is like You, Master of mighty acts,
and who compares to You,
King Who causes death and restores life
and causes salvation to sprout?
And You are faithful to bring the dead to life.
Blessed are You,
Lord Who brings the dead to life.

A traditional prayer from the central portion of the Jewish daily liturgy

Holy art Thou, O God, the universals' Father.

Holy art Thou, O God, whose Will perfects itself by means of its own Powers.

Holy art Thou, O God, who willeth to be known and are known by Thine own.

Holy art Thou, who did by Word make to consist the things that are.

Holy art Thou, of whom All-nature has been made an Image.

Holy art Thou, whose Form Nature never made.

Holy art Thou, more powerful than all power.

Holy art Thou, transcending all pre-eminence.

Holy Thou art, Thou better than all praise.

Accept my reason's offerings pure, from soul and heart for aye stretched up to Thee, O Thou unutterable, unspeakable, Whose Name naught but the Silence can express.

Give ear to me who pray that I may ne'er of Knowledge fail, Knowledge which is our common being's nature; and fill me with Thy Power, and with this Grace of Thine, that I may give the Light to those in ignorance of the Race, my Brethren, and Thy Sons.

For this cause I believe, and I bear witness; I go to Life and Light.

Blessed art Thou, O Father, Thy Man would holy be as Thou art holy, e'en as Thou gavest him Thy full authority to be.

A hymn from the Poimandres, a gnostic work attributed to Hermes Trismegistus

He is patient, he is not angry.
He sits in silence to pass judgement.
He sees you even when he is not looking.
He stays in a far place—but his eyes are on the
    town.
He stands by his children and lets them succeed.
He causes them to laugh—and they laugh.
Ohoho—the father of laughter.
His eye full of joy.
He rests in the sky like a swarm of bees.
Obtala—who turns blood into children.

A prayer of praise from the Yoruba people of Africa

You climb to the mountains surveying the earth,
You suspend from the heavens the circle of the
    lands.
You care for all the peoples of the lands,
And everything that Ea, king of the counselors, had
    created is entrusted to you.
Whatever has breath you shepherd without
    exception,
You are their keeper in upper and lower regions.
Regularly and without cease you traverse the
    heavens,
Every day you pass over the broad earth. . . .
Shepherd of that beneath, keeper of that above,
You, Shamash, direct, you are the light of
    everything.
You never fail to cross the wide expanse of sea,
The depth of which the Igigi know not.
Shamash, your glare reaches down to the abyss
So that monsters of the deep behold your light. . . .
Among the Igigi there is none who toils but you,
None who is supreme like you in the whole
    pantheon of gods.
At your rising the gods of the land assemble;
Your fierce glare covers the land.
Of all the lands of varied speech,
You know their plans, you scan their way.
The whole of mankind bows to you,
Shamash, the universe longs for your light. . . .

You observe, Shamash, prayer, supplication, and
    benediction,
Obeisance, kneeling, ritual murmurs, and
    prostration.
The feeble man calls you from the hollow of his
    mouth,
The humble, the weak, the afflicted, the poor,
She whose son is captive constantly and unceasingly
    confronts you.
He whose family is remote, whose city is distant,
The shepherd [amid] the terror of the steppe
    confronts you,
The herdsman in warfare, the keeper of sheep
    among enemies.
Shamash, there confronts you the caravan, those
    journeying in fear,
The travelling merchant, the agent who is carrying
    capital.
Shamash, there confronts you the fisherman with
    his net,
The hunter, the bowman who drives the game,
With his bird net the fowler confronts you.
The prowling thief, the enemy of Shamash,
The marauder along the tracks of the steppe
    confronts you.
The roving dead, the vagrant soul,
They confront you, Shamash, and you hear all.

Which are the mountains not clothed with your
    beams?
Which are the regions not warmed by the
    brightness of your light?
Brightener of gloom, illuminator of darkness,
Dispeller of darkness, illuminator of the broad earth.

An ancient Babylonian hymn for Shamash, the sun god

God
You define the day with light
You divide the stars from darkness by their light
The green shoots climb toward light
Leaves open to face the light
The human heart yearns for your light
Yours is limitless light,
Abundant,
Boundless,
Worlds thrill to the touch of your light
As the lover thrills to the touch of the beloved.

Wayne Lee Jones

Cover my earth mother four times with many
    flowers.
Cover the heavens with high-piled clouds.
Cover the earth with fog.
Cover the earth with rains.
Cover the earth with lightnings.
Let thunder drum over all the earth.
Let thunder be heard.
Let thunder drum over all the six directions of the
    earth.

A prayer of the Zuni nation of the American Southwest

The mother bird goes early in the morning for food.
The chicks, hungry, wait for her coming.
Just so my heart longs for Thee.
Day and night I think of Thy feet.
The infant calf is tied at home, O God!
In its heart it is calling to its mother.
Says Nama, "Thou art my close friend, O Keshava,
Do not turn me away, O Protector-of-the-helpless."

A prayer by the Hindu poet Namdev

Innumerable are those who pray and adore God.

Innumerable are the religious practices and
austerities.

Innumerable are those who recite the sacred books.

Innumerable are those who remain detached, with
their minds turned away from the world.

Innumerable are the devotees immersed in
knowledge and wisdom.

Innumerable are the men given to benevolence and
charity.

Innumerable are the warriors who match their
strength with steel.

Innumerable are the men who take a vow of silence
and go in trance.

What power have I to describe Your creation?

What power have I to praise it?

Whatever pleases You, that is best,

O, You, Eternal, Abiding, Formless One!

A hymn from the Japji, *a text of the Sikhs*

Remember the circle of the sky
the stars and the brown eagle
the supernatural winds
breathing night and day
from the four directions.

Remember the great life of the sun
breathing on the earth
it lies upon the earth
to bring out life upon the earth
life covering the earth.

Remember the sacredness of things
running streams and dwellings
the young within the nest
a hearth for sacred fire
the holy flame of fire.

A prayer of the Pawnee tribe of the Great Plains

Happy are those who dwell in Your house; may they
always praise You!

Happy is the people for whom this is so,

Happy is the people whose God is the Lord.

I will exalt You, my God the King, and I will bless
Your Name forever and ever.

I will bless You every day, and I will laud Your
Name forever and ever.

The Lord is great and exceedingly praised, and His
greatness is beyond investigation.

Each generation will praise Your deeds to the next
and they will tell of Your mighty deeds.

I will relate the splendid glory of Your power and
Your wondrous deeds.

And they will speak of Your awesome power, and I
will tell of Your greatness.

They will utter a remembrance of Your awesome
goodness, and sing exultantly of Your
righteousness.

The Lord is gracious and merciful, slow to anger,
and great in kindness.

The Lord is good to all; His mercies are on all His
works.

All Your works shall thank You, Lord, and Your
devout ones will bless You.

They will speak of the glory of Your kingdom, and
they will tell of Your power,

To inform human beings of His mighty deeds, and
the glorious splendour of His kingdom.
Your kingdom is a kingdom spanning all eternities,
and Your dominion is throughout every
generation.
The Lord supports all the fallen ones and straightens
all the bent.
The eyes of all look to You with hope and You give
them their food in its proper time;
You open Your hand, and satisfy the desire of every
living thing.
Righteous is the Lord in all His ways and generous
in all His deeds.
The Lord is close to all who call upon Him—to all
who call upon Him sincerely.
He will do the will of those who fear Him; He will
hear their cry and save them.
The Lord protects all who love Him; but He will
destroy all the wicked.
May my mouth declare the praise of the Lord and
may all flesh bless His Holy Name forever and
ever.
We will bless God from this time and forever,
Hallelujah!

Psalm 145, which introduces the Jewish afternoon liturgy

Tambourines!
Tambourines!
Tambourines!
To the glory of God!
Tambourines
To glory!

A gospel shout
And a gospel song:
Life is short
But God is long!

Tambourines!
Tambourines!
Tambourines!
To glory!

Langston Hughes

God
I can speak only in words
I can pray only in words
I can think only in words

But you do not speak in words
Your voice is the expansion of space
Your voice is the progression of time
You speak in the blossoming of flowers
In springs followed by winters followed by springs
Your voice is creation and destruction
The rise and fall of the tides

I can speak only in words

How will You hear my words above the crash of
    thunder
Above the splitting of mountains
Above the screaming multitudes of birds and beasts
Above the countless voices of men speaking also in
    words?
I can speak only in words
Yet you hear behind them
You give me what I need
Forgiving what I ask and what I forget to ask

Wayne Lee Jones

On a dark night,
With longings, by love inflamed,
O happy venture!
I went out unnoticed,
My house being at rest.

In darkness and secure
By the secret ladder, disguised,
O happy venture!
In darkness and in concealment,
My house being at rest.

In the happy night,
In secret, when no one saw me,
Nor did I see anyone,
With neither a light nor a guide
Except the one which burned in my heart.

This light guided me
More certainly than the light of noon
To where He awaited me,
Well I knew Who,
To a place where no one appeared.

O night that guided me!
O night more lovely than dawn!
O night that joined
Beloved with lover,
Lover in the Beloved transformed!

On my flowery breast,
Which I kept for Him alone,
There He remained, sleeping,
And I caressed Him,
And the waving of the cedars made a breeze.

The breeze blew from the tower
As I parted His locks,
With His gentle hand
He wounded my neck,
And suspended all of my senses.

I remained, and I was lost,
I lay my face down on the Beloved,
Everything ceased and I left myself,
I left my cares
Lost among the lilies.

A recital rehearsing the mystical experience of St. John of the Cross, from his Dark
Night of the Soul

The Lord is my pace-setter, I shall not rush;
he makes me stop and rest for quiet intervals,
he provides me with images of stillness,
which restore my serenity.
He leads me in the way of efficiency,
through calmness of mind;
and his guidance is peace.
Even though I have a great many things to
      accomplish each day
I will not fret, for his presence is here.
His timelessness, his all-importance will keep me in
      balance.
He prepares refreshment and renewal
in the midst of activity,
by anointing my mind with his oils of tranquility;
my cup of joyous energy overflows.
Surely harmony and effectiveness shall be
the fruits of my hours
and I shall walk in the pace of my Lord,
and dwell in his house for ever.

"Psalm 23 for Busy People" by Toki Miyashina

Lovely face,
majestic face,
face of beauty,
face of flame,
the face of the Lord God of Israel
when He sits upon His throne of glory,
robed in praise upon His seat of splendour.
His beauty surpasses the beauty of the aged,
His splendour outshines the splendour of
newly-weds in their bridal chamber.

A Jewish mystical ascent hymn

Master! for there is none like thee!

For thy devotees Thou dost choose the best: and
though we ask for brass Thou givest gold.

The hungry Thou dost feed with good things; the
thirsty go to Thee for nectar; and to the naked
Thou dost give shining robes of love.

There is no one, Master, like Thee for us!

As the cow keeps by her calf, so art Thou ever with
Thine own:

Thou, O gracious Lord, dost honour even humble
offerings. Thy loving hand is outstretched to
receive a straw, if only true love doth offer it!

All-generous! All-wise! according to Thy riches
Thou dost satisfy our needs:

In the day of affliction Thou dost hasten to help us,
to make suffering pleasant.

Thou art ever faithful to Thy promises.

There is no one like Thee for us, my Master!

Surdas, a poet from the Hindu tradition

Blessed is the spot,
and the house,
and the place,
and the city,
and the heart,
and the mountain,
and the refuge,
and the cave,
and the valley,
and the land,
and the sea,
and the island,
and the meadow
where mention of God hath been made,
and His praise glorified.

A prayer of Bahá'u'lláh, the founder of the Bahá'í faith

In the Name of the Father, and of the Son, and of
the Holy Spirit.
Amen.

I will go up to the altar of God;
to God, who gladdens my youth.

Judge me, God, and distinguish my place from that of
a people impious; rescue me from the wicked and
deceitful foe.
Because you are my strength, God; why have you
pushed me away, and why do I walk in sorrow,
while the enemy afflicts me?
Send forth your light and your truth: these will
accompany me, and lead me up to your holy
mountain, and into your sanctuary.

And I will go up to the altar of God;
to God, who gladdens my youth.

I will confess to you on a lyre, God, my God; why are
you downcast, my soul, and why do you disturb
me?
Hope in God, especially now that I will confess to
him; and my God is the salvation of my
countenance.
Glory to the Father, and to the Son, and to the Holy
Spirit.

As it was in the beginning, and is now, and will
    always be, world without end.
Amen.

I will go up to the altar of God;
to God, who gladdens my youth.

The introduction to the Latin Mass of the Roman Catholic Church

I am an absolutely true human being,
Who knows that religious rites cause a baby to be
    born,
And knows that which is dangerous,
And knows how to sacrifice in order that it may
    rain.
To convince you that I am a human being in-and-
    out,
I know that a barren wife
Can give birth when rites are performed,
And know that things are harmful;
And I know that worshipping God
Makes it rain when there is a drought.

A credo of the Akamba people of Africa

God is the greatest.

I witness that there is no god but God.

I witness that Muhammad is the messenger of God.

Come to prayer.

Come to your Good.

God is the greatest.

There is no god but God.

O God, glorified, worthy of praise,

blessed is Your name and exalted Your majesty.

There is no god worthy of worship except You.

I seek refuge in God from the outcast Satan.

In the Name of God, the Beneficent, the Merciful.

Praise is for God, Lord of the Worlds,

the Beneficent, the Merciful.

King of the Day of Judgment,

You alone we worship and to You alone we turn for
help.

Guide us in the straight path,

the path of those whom You looked favorably upon,

and who did not incite Your anger

or go astray.

A form of the Muslim call to prayer

Master of the universe,
Who ruled before any form was created,
At the time when His will brought all into being—
Then His Name was proclaimed as King.
After all has ceased to be, He,
The Awesome One, will reign alone.
It is He Who was,
He Who is,
and He Who shall remain, in splendour.
He is One—
There is no second to compare to Him,
To declare as His equal.
Without beginning, without end—
He is the power and dominion.
He is my God, my living Redeemer,
Rock of my pain in time of distress.
He is my banner,
And refuge for me,
The portion in my cup on the day I call.
Into His hand I will entrust my spirit when I go to
       sleep—
And I shall awaken!
My body shall remain with my spirit.
The Lord is with me,
I shall not fear.

A traditional Jewish hymn

PRAYERS

OF

THANKSGIVING

O God,
we thank you for this earth, our home;
for the wide sky and the blessed sun,
for the salt sea and the running water,
for the everlasting hills and the never-resting winds,
for trees and the common grass underfoot.
We thank you for our senses
by which we hear the songs of birds,
and see the splendour of the summer fields,
and taste of the autumn fruits,
and rejoice in the feel of the snow,
and smell the breath of the spring.
Grant us a heart wide open to all this beauty;
and save our souls from being so blind
that we pass unseeing when even the common
    thornbush
is aflame with your glory, O God our Creator,
who lives and reigns for ever and ever.

A prayer of Walter Rauschenbusch

Listen, O fortunate ones, to my joyful song,
That all my desires have been fulfilled.
I have obtained God, the Supreme Being,
And all my griefs have disappeared.
My sorrows, afflictions, and sufferings have departed
By listening to the true Word.
The saints and the holy are filled with joy,
When they hear the Word from the perfect
     Preceptor.
He who hears the Word is made pure,
He who speaks is made holy,
The Eternal Preceptor will fill their hearts.
I proclaim, for those who attach themselves to the
     Enlightener's feet,
The heavenly music plays.

From the Japji, a text of the Sikhs

When have we ever forgotten to make sacrifices to
    you and to enumerate your honourable names?
Why are you so miserly?
If you do not improve, we will let all your
    honourable names fall into oblivion.
What will your fate be then!
You will have to go and feed on locusts.
Improve: else we forget you.
For whose good is it that we make sacrifices and
    celebrate the praises?
You bring us neither harvests nor abundant herds.
You show no gratitude whatever for all the trouble
    we take.
However, we do not wish to estrange ourselves
    completely from you
and we will say to other men that we do not
    completely possess the spirits of our forebears.
You will suffer from it.
We are angry with you.

A prayer of the Zulu people of South Africa

Lord, these are such little things for which we pray.
If someone were to ask them of me, I could do
      them as well.
But you are a hundred times more able than I and
      even more willing,
so if we asked you for something greater, you could
      still give it—
and the more willingly the greater it is that we ask for.

A prayer of the Christian mystic Meister Eckhart

In beauty you shall be my representation.
In beauty you shall be my song.
In beauty you shall be my medicine.
In beauty my holy medicine.

A prayer of the Navajo tribe of the American Southwest

He that dwelleth in the secret place of the most
      High shall abide under the shadow of the
      Almighty.

I will say of the Lord, He is my refuge and my
      fortress: my God; in Him will I trust.

Surely He shall deliver thee from the snare of the
      fowler, and from the noisome pestilence.

He shall cover thee with His feathers, and under His
      wings shalt thou trust: His truth shall be thy
      shield and buckler.

Thou shalt not be afraid of the terror by night; nor
      for the arrow that flieth by day;

Nor for the pestilence that walketh in darkness; nor
      for the destruction that wasteth at noonday.

A thousand shall fall at thy side, and ten thousand at
      thy right hand; but it shall not come nigh thee.

Only with thine eyes shalt thou behold and see the
      reward of the wicked.

Because thou hast made the Lord, which is my
      refuge, even the most High, thy habitation;
      There shall no evil befall thee, neither shall any
      plague come nigh thy dwelling.

For He shall give his angels charge over thee, to
      keep thee in all thy ways.

They shall bear thee up in their hands, lest thou
      dash thy foot against a stone.

Thou shalt tread upon the lion and adder: the young
lion and the dragon shalt thou trample under
feet.
Because he hath set his love upon me, therefore will I
deliver him: I will set him on high, because he
hath known my name.
He shall call upon me and I will answer him: I will
be with him in trouble; I will deliver him, and
honour him.
With long life will I satisfy him, and shew him my
salvation.

Psalm 91, attributed magical properties in Jewish folklore

i thank You God for most this amazing
day:for the leaping greenly spirits of trees
and a blue true dream of sky;and for everything
which is natural which is infinite which is yes

(i who have died am alive again today,
and this is the sun's birthday;this is the birth
day of life and of love and of wings:and of the gay
great happening illimitably earth)

how should tasting touching hearing seeing
breathing any—lifted from the no
of all nothing—human merely being
doubt unimaginable You?

(now the ears of my ears awake and
now the eyes of my eyes are opened)

e. e. cummings

Lord!
Where was I?
Oh yes! This flower, this sun,
thank you! Your world is beautiful!
This scent of roses . . .
Where was I?
A drop of dew
rolls to sparkle in a lily's heart.
I have to go . . .
Where? I do not know!
The wind has painted fancies
on my wings.
Fancies . . .
Where was I?
Oh yes! Lord,
I had something to tell you:
Amen.

"The Prayer of the Butterfly," by Carmen Bernos de Gasztold

We return thanks to our mother, the earth, which
sustains us.

We return thanks to the rivers and streams, which
supply us with water.

We return thanks to all herbs, which furnish
medicines for the cure of our diseases.

We return thanks to the corn, and to her sisters, the
beans and squashes, which give us life.

We return thanks to the bushes and trees, which
provide us with fruit.

We return thanks to the wind, which, moving the
air, has banished diseases.

We return thanks to the moon and stars, which have
given to us their light when the sun was gone.

We return thanks to our grandfather, He'no, that he
has protected his grandchildren from witches
and reptiles, and has given to us his rain.

We return thanks to the sun, that he has looked
upon the earth with a beneficent eye.

Lastly, we return thanks to the Great Spirit, in
whom is embodied all goodness, and who
directs all things for the good of his children.

A prayer of the Iroquois tribe of the Eastern Woodlands

Lord,
I thank you for the sweet taste of the apple
and for the fertility of the branch
and for the solid majesty of the limb
and for the firm support of the trunk.
I thank you for the searching thirst of the root
and for the life-giving powers of the water
and for the nourishing qualities of the soil
and for the yellow warmth of the sun.
I thank you for the yearning of the seed to grow
and before the seed, for the shade of older trees,
and before the trees, for the spinning of the world
        into cohesion,
and before the world, for the womb of black space.
And you alone are to be thanked.
And you alone are the source of all that is.
And all the sweet tastes
and all who taste of the sweet tastes
emerge from you
as apples emerge from the living branches
of apple trees.

Wayne Lee Jones

My Lord, for the other clarity
that you have given my soul,
I thank you.

My Lord, for the tranquility
that you have given my soul,
I thank you.

My Lord, night has come
You close my eyes before the day
And me, I'll paint once again
Paintings for you
On the earth and in the sky.

Marc Chagall

Thank you, God,
for unions:
for the union of fingers in one hand
and of limbs in one body;
for the union of mother, father, and child in one
        family
and of human beings in one community;
for the union of lovers in one love
and of all loves in your love;
for the union of yesterday with tomorrow
and of actions with their consequences.
Thank you, God,
for the union of heart and mind
and of body and spirit.
You are the One
who conceals unity
within distinct parts.

Wayne Lee Jones

I thank You, Lord, for knowing me better than I
    know myself,
And for letting me know myself better than others
    know me.
Make me, I pray to You, better than they suppose,
And forgive me for what they do not know.

A personal prayer of Abu Bakr, the first Caliph of Islam

Index of First Lines

Acknowledgments

The title of this book is a phrase from the poem, "Song of the Sky Loom." The complete poem from *Songs of the Tewa* by Herbert Joseph Spinden, and this phrase appear courtesy of Sunstone Press, Box 2321, Santa Fe, NM 87504-2321.

p. 2   Original work of the author.

p. 3   The poem, "Song of the Sky Loom" from *Songs of the Tewa* by Herbert Joseph Spinden appears courtesy of Sunstone Press, Box 2321, Santa Fe, NM 87504-2321.

p. 4   *The Sublime Path of the Victorious Ones*. Dharamsala: Library of Tibetan Works and Archives.

p. 14   Dakota, found in Stoddard, Sandol. *Prayers, Praises and Thanksgivings*. New York: Dial Books, 1992.

p. 16 (*top*)   From *Peace on Earth: A Book of Prayers from Around the World* by Bijou Le Tord, Editor. Copyright Collection, Adaptations, and illustrations © 1992 ed., Bijou Le Tord. Used by permission of Delacorte Press, a division of Bantam Double-day Dell Publishing Group, Inc.

p. 17   Barrett, L. D. *The Path of Light*. London: John Murray, Ltd. Reprinted by permission of John Murray, Ltd.

p. 18   Abbott, Justin E., trans. *Strotramala: A Garland of Hindu Prayers*. Scottish Mission Industries, Ltd., 1929.

p. 19   Reprinted from *Prayers for Dark People*, by W. E. B. Du Bois, ed. Herbert Aptheker (Amherst: University of Massachusetts Press, 1980), © 1980 by The University of Massachusetts Press.

pp. 20–21   *The Sublime Path of the Victorious Ones*. Dharamsala: Library of Tibetan Works and Archives. Reprinted by permission of the Library of Tibetan Works and Archives.

p. 22 (*top*)   "Bedouin Prayer at Sunset."   Greene, Barbara and Gollancz, Victor.   *God of a Hundred Names*. London: Victor Gollancz Limited.   All attempts at tracing the original copyright holder of "Bedouin Prayer at Sunset" were unsuccessful.

pp. 24–25   Reprinted from *Black Elk Speaks*, by John G. Neihardt, by permission of the University of Nebraska Press.   Copyright 1932, 1959, 1972, by John G. Neihardt.   © 1961 by the John G. Neihardt Trust.

p. 26–27   revised from Griffith, Ralph T. H.   *The Hymns of the Rgveda*. Vol II. Varanasi: The Chowkhamba Sanskrit Series Office, 1889.   pp. 138-139.

p. 30 (*bottom*)   Marshall, Lorna, ed. "Kung Bushman Religious Beliefs." *Africa*. Vol. 32. London: Oxford University Press, 1962.

pp. 32–33   Excerpt from *The Nectar of Chanting*, pp. 63-64, (New York: SYDA Foundation), © 1975, 1983, 1984.   All rights reserved.   Reprinted by permission.

pp. 34–35   DiNola, Alfonso M.   "Hymn to the Thunderbird." *The Prayers of Man*. William Heinemann, Ltd., 1962.

p. 38   Wellman, Esther, trans., in Fleming, Daniel J. *The World at One in Prayer.* New York: Harper & Brothers Publishers, 1942.

p. 39   Original work of the author.

pp. 40–41   *The Sublime Path of the Victorious Ones.* Dharamsala: Library of Tibetan Works and Archives. Reprinted by permission of the Library of Tibetan Works and Archives.

p. 42   Hoyland, John S. *A Book of Prayers, Written for Use in an Indian College.* London: The Challenge, Ltd.

p. 43   Selection from *In the Trail of the Wind: American Indian Poems and Ritual Orations,* ed. John Bierhorst. © 1971 by John Bierhorst. Reprinted by permission of Farrar, Straus & Giroux Inc.

p. 44   Harlow, Ralph S. *Prayers for Times Like These.* Association Press, 1942.

pp. 46–47   From Jackson, Kenneth H. "The Wish of Manchan of Liath." *A Celtic Miscellany.* London: Routledge & Kegan Paul, 1972.

p. 48 *(top)*   "The Commonest Shinto Prayer." Greene, Barbara and Gollancz, Victor. *God of a Hundred*

Names. London: Victor Gollancz Limited. All attempts at tracing the original copyright holder of "The Commonest Shinto Prayer" were unsuccessful.

p. 50   Reproduced from Alexander Carmichael, *Carmina Gadelica*-Volume 111 with the permission of the Trustees and the Publishers, The Scottish Academic Press.

p. 51   Desai, Bejon N. and Khan, Roni K. *Homage unto Asho Zarathustra*. Navaz Publications, 1993.

pp. 52–53   Drinkwater, John. *The Complete Poems of John Drinkwater*. London: Samuel French, Ltd.

pp. 54–55   Abbott, Justin E., trans. *Strotramala: A Garland of Hindu Prayers*. Scottish Mission Industries, Ltd., 1929.

p. 56   "The Prayer of the Ox," from *Prayers from the Ark* by Carmen Bernos de Gasztold, translated by Rumer Godden, Translation © 1962, renewed 1990 by Rumer Godden. Original Copyright 1947, © 1955 by Editions du Cloitre. Used by permission of Viking Penguin, a division of Penguin Books USA Inc.

p. 57   Hoyland, John S. *An Indian Peasant Mystic*. Prinit Press, 1978.

p. 69   Shackle, Christopher and Moir, Zawahir. *Ismaili Hymns from South Asia*. London: School of Oriental and African Studies, 1992. Reprinted by permission of the School of Oriental and African Studies.

p. 70   Original work of the author.

p. 71   Satow, Ernest. "Ancient Japanese Rituals." *Transactions of the Asiatic Society of Japan*. Vol. 7, Part I. Yokohama: The Society, 1879.

p. 73   Montague, James, ed. "The Acts of John." *The Apocryphal New Testament*. London: Oxford University Press, 1993.

p. 74   Nketia, J. H. *Drumming in the Akan Communities of Ghana*. Accra: University of Ghana, 1963.

p. 76   Mead, G. R. S. *Thrice Greatest Hermes*. Vol. I. London: The Theosophical Publishing Society, 1906. p. 12.

p. 77   Beier, Ulli. *African Poetry*. Cambridge: Cambridge University Press, 1966. Reprinted with the permission of Cambridge University Press.

pp. 78–80 Lambert, W. G. *Babylonian Wisdom Literature*. London: Oxford University Press, 1960.

p. 81   Original work of the author.

p. 82   Stevenson, Matilda Coxe. "The Zuni Indians." *23rd Annual BAE Report*. Washington, D.C.: Government Printing Office, 1904.

p. 83   Abbott, Justin E., trans. *Strotramala: A Garland of Hindu Prayers*. Scottish Mission Industries, Ltd., 1929.

p. 85   Fletcher. *22nd Annual BAE Report*. Washington, D.C.: Government Printing Office, 1903.

p. 88   From *Collected Poems* by Langston Hughes. © 1994 by the Estate of Langston Hughes. Reprinted by permission of Alfred A. Knopf, Inc.

p. 89   Original work of the author.

p. 92   Toki Miyashina. "Psalm 23 for Busy People."

p. 93   Carmi, T., ed. "The Face of God." *The Penguin Book of Hebrew Verse*. London: Penguin Books, 1981.

p. 95   Bahá'í Prayers, Copyright 1954, © 1982, 1985, 1991, by the National Spiritual Assembly of the Bahá'ís of the United States.

p. 98   Mbiti, John S. *The Prayers of African Religion*. Orbis Books.

p. 104   DiNola, A. M. *The Prayers of Man*. London: William Heinemann, Ltd., 1962. Reprinted by permission of William Heinemann, Ltd.

p. 105   Matthews, Washington. "The Night Chant, A Navajo Ceremony." *Memoirs of the American Museum of Natural History*. Vol. VI. Washington, D.C.: Smithsonian Institution, 1902.

p. 108   "i thank You God for most this amazing," copyright 1950, © 1978, 1991 by the Trustees for the E. E. Cummings Trust. Copyright © 1979 by George James Firmage, from *Complete Poems: 1904-1962* by E. E. Cummings, Edited by George J. Firmage. Reprinted by permission of Liveright Publishing Corporation.

p. 109   "The Prayer of the Butterfly," from *Prayers from the Ark* by Carmen Bernos de Gasztold, trans. Rumer Godden. Translation copyright © 1962, renewed 1990 by Rumer Godden. Original copyright 1947, © 1955 by Editions du Cloitre. Used by permission of Viking Penguin, a division of Penguin Books USA Inc.

p. 110   Lewis, Morgan, trans., in Parker, Ely S. *League of the Ho-De-No-Sau-Nee*. 1851. pp. 202-203.

p. 111   Original work of the author.

p. 112   From *Peace on Earth: A Book of Prayers from Around the World* by Bijou Le Tord, Editor. Copyright Collection, Adaptations, and illustrations © 1992 by Bijou Le Tord. Used by permission of Delacorte Press, a division of Bantam Doubleday Dell Publishing Group, Inc.

p. 113   Original work of the author.